The K-Nine Chronicles:

Rex Finds a Home

Carliss Maddox

To order additional copies of this book, contact:
Xlibris
844-714-8691
www.Xlibris.com
Orders@Xlibris.com

ISBN: Softcover   979-8-3694-0749-3
       EBook   979-8-3694-0748-6

Print information available on the last page

Rev. date: 11/15/2023

The K-Nine Chronicles:

Rex Finds a Home

The Mason family lived in a small town in Oklahoma. Oklahoma is a quiet place full of endless fields of green grass, clear skies, and prairie dogs. People from Oklahoma are very friendly. Everyone waves to each other, even if they do not know you.

Mr. Mason was a Sergeant in the United States Army. He traveled all the time. He wore a military uniform to work every day. Mrs. Mason was an elementary school teacher. She always greeted Mr. Mason with a hug, a smile, and a home-cooked meal when he came home from work.

One day Mr. Mason, knowing his wife's love for animals, decided to buy her a puppy. He visited many animal shelters. In the shelters, he passed by many kennels with dogs in them. He saw all kinds of dogs. He saw big dogs and little dogs. He saw dogs with lots of hair and dogs with very little hair. He saw dogs who were happy and wagging their tails. He also saw dogs who looked sad and never once looked up from their kennels.

Despite his efforts, he did not find that special dog he was looking for, which made him very sad. However, Mr. Mason was not going to give up his search for the perfect dog. He got into his car and drove around town, visiting other animal shelters to find the right dog for his family.

As Mr. Mason was turning a corner, he heard barking noises in the distance. He decided to follow the barking noises to see where it would lead. As he continued driving, he came upon an animal shelter covered up by two large willow oak trees. There was a large sign on the building that read, "Second Chance Animal Shelter."

A bell chimed when Mr. Mason walked into the shelter. In the distance, he saw a very old, wise-looking man whose hair and beard were white as snow. The man was busy talking to two puppies in a kennel, wrestling with each other over the dog food.

The old man called out to them, "Heeeyyyy!
There is no need to fight each other!"

The old man turned and noticed Mr. Mason walking toward him and asked him, "Can I help you?" Mr. Mason said, "I am looking for a puppy for my family. I have been looking all over town and I haven't been able to find the right dog."

17

The old man replied, "Nice to meet you. I'm the owner of the shelter. What kind of dog are you looking for?"

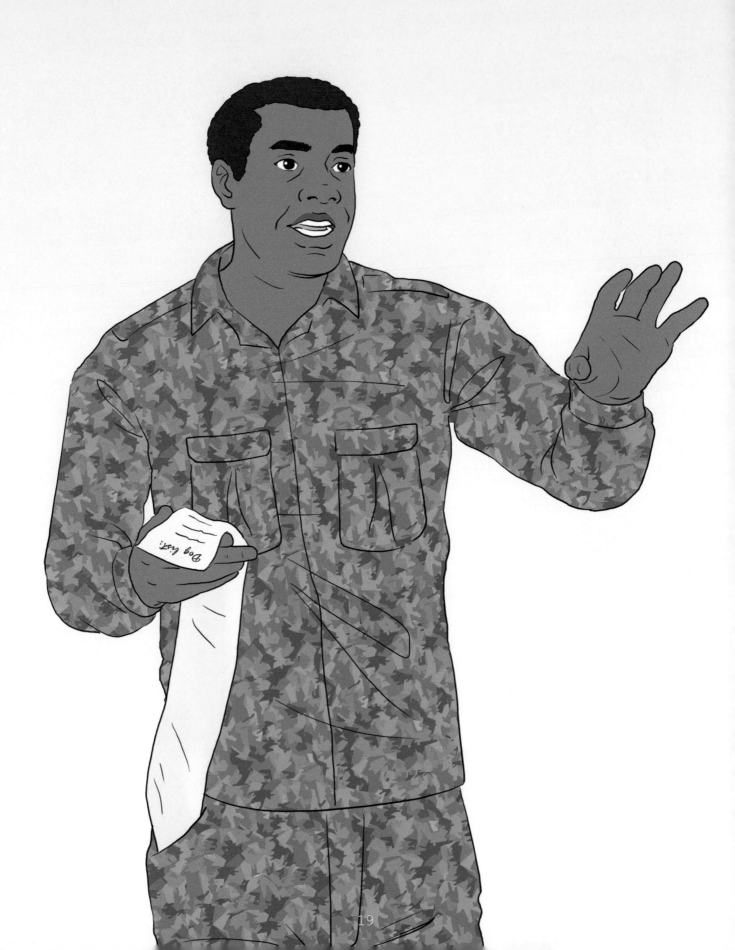

Mr. Mason pulled a long piece of paper out of his pocket with a list of all the things he was looking for in a dog. He said, "I am looking for a dog who won't grow too big, doesn't tear up the furniture, knows how to sit and stay on command, doesn't pee in the house, doesn't do a lot of barking but will bark if someone is trying to hurt us, and also......... ."

The old man interrupted him and said, "Oh, I see your dilemma. You have been looking for the perfect dog. Good luck with your search. All dogs have things about them that are good and some things that are not so good."

"The dog you find may not tear up the furniture but will eat your favorite pair of shoes for its afternoon snack."

"Your dog may not bark as much as your neighbor's dog but lets out a long and loud howl whenever it hears the sirens of a fire truck or police car."

"While your dog may know how to sit and come when you call him, he may not understand the command "stop" when he chases children down the street. You see, you will still have problems no matter what dog you choose. You will just have to love him even though he may do things that are not so good. We are not perfect. What makes you think you can find a perfect dog?" Mr. Mason replied, "I never looked at it that way."

The old man took him to the kennel of the two puppies that were fighting each other. He said, "Look at these two puppies." As Mr. Mason looked through the kennel, his eyes were drawn to an adorable scruffy-looking puppy with playful eyes. His tail curled over his back. His hair was short. He was a salt and pepper color all over his body except for the front of his mouth. His mouth was white at the top and bottom, which made him look like he had a white beard. He had big beautiful brown eyes. "What a cute little puppy," said Mr. Mason.

The old man said, "Yes. He's a playful little dog. This dog may seem aggressive, but he's a sweet dog with a big heart. You really can't judge a dog by what you see on the outside." "What kind of dog is he?" asked Mr. Mason. "This dog is a mix of the Chihuahua and Shih Tzu breed," said the old man.

Suddenly, the salt and pepper dog stopped fighting and looked up at Mr. Mason with his big, brown eyes as if to say hello. Mr. Mason took one look at him and told the shelter owner, "I'll take him!"

After Mr. Mason spoke those words, the puppy put his paw through the bars of the kennel to touch him while the other dog looked on. Mr. Mason reached out and touched his little paw and said, "Hey, little fella. I'm going to take you home!" The dog seemed to understand the word "home" because he started wagging his tail and running around the kennel.

The old man took the dog out of the kennel and gave him to Mr. Mason to hold. The dog licked his face so much that it started to shine against the rays of sunlight coming into the shelter.

The old man said, "You made a wise decision to pick this dog. When this dog was born, he was the smallest in the litter, and his mother didn't want him. The owner thought the puppy would die because he was so small. They dropped him off here, hoping someone would save him. You, Mr. Mason, are giving him a second chance." The shelter owner asked, "What are you going to call him?" Mr. Mason thought for a moment and then replied, "I will call him Rex."

Mr. Mason paid the shelter owner, signed the papers, put Rex on his shoulder, and headed out the door. Rex looked back at the shelter. As the door opened and closed, the door chime went off for the last time, at least in Rex's mind. Rex knew he was going on a journey that would change his life forever.

Printed in the United States
by Baker & Taylor Publisher Services